better together*

* This book is best read together, grownup and kid.

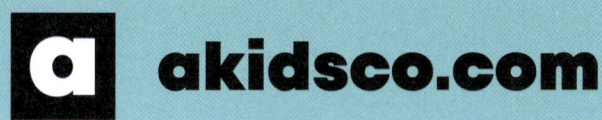 akidsco.com

a
kids
book
about

children & FAMILIES first

a
kids
book
about

Foster Families

by Children & Families First

A Kids Co.
Editor Emma Wolf
Designer Jelani Memory
Creative Director Rick DeLucco
Studio Manager Kenya Feldes
Sales Director Melanie Wilkins
Head of Books Jennifer Goldstein
CEO and Founder Jelani Memory

DK
Delhi Technical Team Bimlesh Tiwary Pushpak Tyagi, Rakesh Kumar
Senior Production Editor Jennifer Murray
Senior Production Controller Louise Minihane
Senior Acquisitions Editor Katy Flint
Acquisitions Project Editor Sara Forster
Managing Art Editor Vicky Short
Managing Director, Licensing Mark Searle

First American edition, 2025
Published in the United States by DK Publishing, 1745 Broadway, 20th Floor,
New York, NY 10019

First published in Great Britain in 2025 by
Dorling Kindersley Limited, 20 Vauxhall Bridge Road, London SW1V 2SA
A Penguin Random House Company

The authorised representative in the EEA is
Dorling Kindersley Verlag GmbH. Arnulfstr. 124, 80636 Munich, Germany

A catalog record for this book is available from the Library of Congress.
A CIP catalogue record for this book is available from the British Library.
ISBN: 978-0-2417-4382-9

DK books are available at special discounts when purchased in bulk for sales
promotions, premiums, fund-raising, or education use. For details, contact:
DK Publishing Special Markets, 1745 Broadway, 20th Floor, New York, NY 10019
SpecialSales@dk.com

Printed and bound in China
www.dk.com
akidsco.com

MIX
Paper | Supporting
responsible forestry
FSC™ C018179

This book was made with Forest
Stewardship Council™ certified
paper – one small step in DK's
commitment to a sustainable future.
**Learn more at www.dk.com/uk/
information/sustainability**

This book is dedicated to all members of the foster family constellation—especially foster parents, foster siblings, and children experiencing foster care.

Thank you to the amazing foster families who provide endless support to children.

Author proceeds from sales of this book support the work of Children & Families First.

Intro
for grownups

What is the role of a foster family? Whether you are a foster parent (or considering becoming one), part of a foster family, a child experiencing foster care, or another community member, this book will help clarify and answer some questions about what it means to be a part of a foster family.

Foster families make sure kids feel cared for, safe, and loved. This experience involves a variety of emotions for everyone involved, whether they are part of the foster family or connected in another way. We hope this book offers an opportunity for further conversations about grief, loss, change, growth, and resiliency.

What is a foster family?

A foster family...

- protects and nurtures kids.

- keeps kids safe.

- walks alongside kids on their journey through life.

- makes a commitment to being a meaningful part of a kid's life.

Why are foster families needed?

Unfortunately, not all grownups
are able to care for their kids.

Sometimes, grownups have big challenges they need to work on.

This doesn't mean they're bad people. Or that they don't love or want to take care of their kids.

But sometimes, while they're getting help, their kids will live with a foster family.

It may be for a short time.

It may be for a long time.

Some kids may stay with several different foster families.

Even after their grownups get help, it may not be safe for a kid to live with them again.

In that situation, the foster care system can also help kids join a different, permanent family.

Joining a foster family
might feel scary.

For some kids, joining a foster family might also feel like a relief.

When a kid joins a foster family, things may be really different from what they're used to...

a new bed,

new smells,

different foods,

moving from a big city to a smaller town (or the other way around),

and maybe the foster family even looks different than they do.

No **2** foster families are the same.

And for kids who join a foster family, we want you to know...

no matter how you feel about this change, what happened was never your fault.

Kids join foster families because of *grownups'* challenges, *not* because kids did anything wrong or because they're bad kids.

Anything a kid feels...

anger, fear, sadness, safety, shyness, joy, confusion, frustration, worry, hope, rejection, reassured, embarrassment, guilt, loneliness, discomfort, shame, happiness, calm,

or any combination of these (or others) is OK.

A foster family listens to what kids are experiencing and helps talk through feelings and emotions about it.

And foster families are there for a lot of other stuff, too.

They include you.

They help you explore your interests.

They help you with your schoolwork.

They provide a safe place for you to sleep.

They take you to a doctor if you're not feeling well.

They offer you comfort when you're feeling sad or worried.

They help you learn how to process your emotions.

They know that often kids want to go back to their biological families, and they'll remind you that's OK.

They help you learn how to work through challenges in a healthy and peaceful way.

They teach you how to care for yourself, and how to know when to ask for help.

They teach you how to work together as a part of a family

(yes, that means cleaning your room).

They want you to enjoy being a kid.

Being part of a foster family means there may be big changes for everyone.

People share their time, space, and things differently.

Finding a new routine can take time, and that transition comes with its own set of challenges.

But it's important to know that
foster families are dedicated to
making things work.

To become a foster family, they had to do *a lot* of work to show their commitment to having new kids join their families.

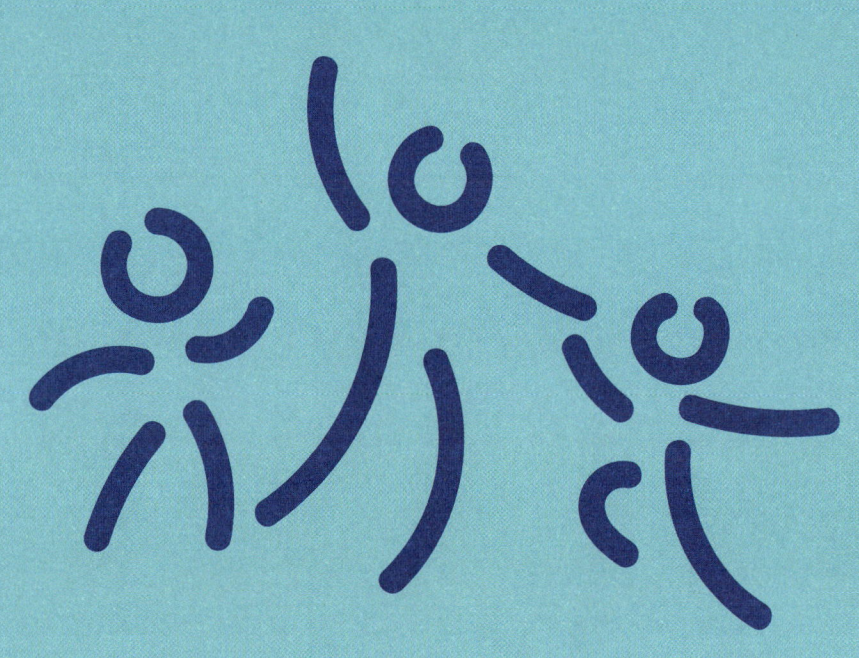

It's a privilege to care for other people's kids.

Foster families are meant to provide a sense of belonging for kids in foster care—regardless of how long they're together.

And if a kid moves on, that foster family may remain an important part of their lives.

Foster families are here to make kids feel safe, loved, protected, and nurtured during this challenging part of their life's journey.

And when that's the case...

Kids can

thrive.

Outro
for grownups

There are over 391,000 children experiencing foster care in the United States today.[1] Oftentimes, people are not aware of how many kids are in need of committed foster families.

Foster families are a valued part of the child welfare team and are essential to our communities. They support kids while birth families learn new and healthy ways to help their own kids flourish.

Maybe this book will lead you to consider becoming a foster parent, or maybe it will clarify your family members' interest in being part of a foster family.

Grownup, please share this resource with the kids in your life—those who are and are not experiencing foster care. We hope this book brings awareness to and normalizes the foster family experience for kids and all families.

[1]"Key Facts and Statistics," National Foster Care Month - Child Welfare Information Gateway, accessed December 1, 2023, https://www.childwelfare.gov/fostercaremonth/awareness/facts/.

About The Contributors

Abby Fischer, LCSW (she/her), has worked in foster care and adoption for 10 years and is a former teacher. She is excited to share this resource with kids and families.

Lynn Fraipont, PhD (she/her), formerly a special education teacher, has worked in foster care and adoption for 13 years. She has 4 sons who joined her family through adoption.

Sandra Korines, LCSW (she/her), has dedicated the last 10 years of her career to foster care and adoption. She's thankful for the privilege to work with foster families every day.

Mike McHugh, MS (he/him), is an adoptive and former foster parent. He has been involved in child welfare for more than 2 decades.

About the Organization

Children & Families First, a nonprofit organization serving
Delaware, has been providing foster care
and adoption services for over a century.

 @cffde   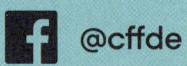 @cffde